G. C Mast

**Primer of the Phonic Method of Teaching Reading & Writing**

**Simeltaneously**

G. C Mast

**Primer of the Phonic Method of Teaching Reading & Writing Simeltaneously**

ISBN/EAN: 9783337003142

Printed in Europe, USA, Canada, Australia, Japan

Cover: Foto ©Paul-Georg Meister /pixelio.de

More available books at **www.hansebooks.com**

# PRIMER

OF

# THE PHONIC METHOD

OF TEACHING

# READING & WRITING SIMULTANEOUSLY

WITH AN

INTRODUCTION.

BY

G. C. MAST,

*Principal of Belgrave College, Pimlico; author of " French: Practice and Theory"; " Linear Drawing"; &c.*

[All rights reserved]

LONDON:
CHARLES BEAN, 81, NEW NORTH ROAD, N.
1875.

# PREFACE.

A GOOD knowledge of *Reading* and *Writing* is generally admitted to be the foundation of all the other branches of knowledge. But it is not so generally understood that upon the manner in which these fundamental arts of education are acquired by the young, their progress in other studies mainly depends. And yet it might appear reasonable enough to suppose that, as the beginning is, so will be the progress and the final result.

"The results of our existing system of primary education" are pronounced by trustworthy authorities to be "a miserable failure." "Education up to the point of reading and writing to any useful purpose under present circumstances is not attained by the great bulk of the population." "It takes from six to seven years to learn the arts of reading and spelling with a fair degree of intelligence." According to the last Report of the Committee of the

Council of Education, out of a hundred pupils "only nine were presented in the fourth and higher standards."\*

The cause of these failures is attributed mainly to the defective alphabet and orthography of the English language. The latter is characterised as "a labyrinth, a chaos, an absurdity, a disgrace to our age,"† and as "a mass of anomalies, the growth of ignorance and chance, equally repugnant to good taste and common sense."‡

What a vicious creature this beautiful English language is represented to be by its friends!

But what if, after all, it should prove to be only a spirited horse, a modern Bucephalus that required nothing more than proper management to be subdued and made willing to obey its leader? Without using whip or spur for guiding it, only by means of bit and bridle, and leading it out of the distorted picture of its own shadow, the Author has succeeded in subduing it, so as to make it subservient to all his wishes.

For years it had been his wish to introduce in this country the *German,* or *Phonic method of teaching reading and writing simultaneously,* not yet, so far as the Author knows, practised in England. But it was not until December last that he had an opportunity of doing so in a lecture which he gave before the College of Pre-

---

\* *Times,* July 1st, 1875.

† Sir C. E. Trevelyan. ‡ The Bishop of St. David's.

ceptors.* The favourable reception the method he advocated met there encouraged him to submit it to a larger circle of teachers and friends of education in the form of this little book. It contains an adaptation of German principles of teaching reading and writing to the English language. The only novelties in it are the " marks "—strokes, ties, dots, and brackets, to the adoption of which the Author was unintentionally driven; but their utility proved, on trial, greater than could have been anticipated. One example of the capacity of this method may suffice.

A girl not quite six years of age being taught by the Author, could read the first part of this book (in manuscript) after less than three months' instruction; the lessons lasting from 10 to 15 minutes daily.

After six months she could read any easy elementary book; and after nine months, any book within the scope of young children; and at the same time she could read letters, received from her little friends, and answer them.

An elder sister of hers, equally intelligent, but having been taught by the prevailing methods, could not read so fluently after three years' toil as her younger sister after nine months' amusement.

A large class of sixty to eighty children could, by any teacher acquainted with this method, be taught with ease *reading and writing*, intelligently, in less than twelve months.

---

* See *Educational Times*, January, 1875.

Should the exposition of the method in the "Introduction" not prove sufficient, the Author would be happy to explain it further before any School Board, or assembly of teachers.

At the same time he would feel obliged for any suggestion for improvements, addressed to him,

THE AUTHOR.

Belgrave College,
148, Buckingham Palace Road, London.
*September*, 1875.

# INTRODUCTION.

The *uncertainty of the sound* of some letters, and the *anomalies of spelling* in English are the chief obstacles to beginners in reading. And whatever may have been done by compilers of reading books in the way of arranging the words in an easy and systematic manner, no feasible method has been produced which, going to the very root of the evils, has succeeded in overcoming them. The attempts to remove them through the introduction of an altogether new or an enlarged alphabet, or through a remodelling of the spelling of the whole language, must fail on account of the double toil these methods entail of first learning quite a new, and then the usual manner of writing and spelling.

No practical man would erect a large mansion to pull it down again as soon as it is finished, and to build of its materials a smaller house for permanent and ordinary use. But it is a usual thing in building to erect a scaffold to facilitate the operations. And that is what the Author has done. In order to reach the difficulties of the English language he has introduced some external means, called here "Marks." For the removal of difficulties arising from the *uncertainty* of the sound of letters he has affixed *strokes*, *dots* and *ties*, either above or below the letters ; and for the removal of those arising from redundancy of letters he has employed the *bracket*. He thus obtained an *ample Phonic alhpabet*, without adding a single new letter, and a *simplified spelling*, without altering the orthography of a single word. As we prepare food for infants, so the English language has been merely *prepared* for the purpose of facilitating the acquisition of the art of reading, and prepared by means which, having served their purpose, can be laid aside as easily as the scaffolding can be taken down when the building is finished, or the leading strings be left off when a child can walk. *English thus prepared* is now in a condition to have principles applied which in Germany are no longer under discussion, but are practised everywhere, underlying every sound method of teaching elementary reading: they consist in *teaching reading phonically and in the closest connection with writing.* In this German method spelling is postponed until a child can read. In teaching reading, instead of the *names* of each consonant only its *phonic value,* power or sound is given; that part, namely, which *sounds together with a vowel in each syllable,* and which we obtain by dropping entirely the *vowel sound of its* name.

The phonic value, for instance, of the letter *b* is obtained by dropping the *ee* of its name; that of *k* by dropping the *ay* of its name, &c. What is left after the dropping of the vowel sound of each consonant is hardly a sound; it becomes one in connection with the vowel of a word or syllable—whence its name *con-sonant* —a letter *sounding with* a vowel. Now, as a means of referring to them the names of the consonants are all necessary; but *spelling* or saying the names of the letters, as a means to teach reading for beginners is not only not necessary, but a grave mistake. For, as a rule, the vowel sounds of the names of the consonants do not tally with those of the words or syllables in which they occur, and must consequently cause confusion in the mind of the young. A few examples will show this clearly. If we take such easy words as *dog, cat, icy,* a child cannot possibly understand that d-o-g, as usually spelt, could sound *dog*; nor c-a-t, cat; nor i-c-y, icy. He will learn the sound of these words not from hearing them spelt, but merely from being told by the teacher, quite mechanically. Far from being pleased to discover a connection between the one and the other, he must be puzzled about the strangeness of this kind of learning; for spelling c-a-t would produce in his mind rather the idea of *see-a-tea*, than *cat*, and spelling i-c-y the idea of *I-see-why* than *icy*. So also o-u-r sounds *oh-you-are*, r-u-n almost *are-you-in ?*, and w-a-x almost *double-you-a-axe ;* worst of all l-a-d might be mistaken for a *lady*.

It is a serious matter thus to disappoint the young with every word they have to spell, but it is a more serious error to expect that children can learn reading easily and intelligently by this method. According to the method proposed, the child would have been taught to pronounce the letters of which *dog, cat, icy, our*, and *run* consist *phonically* and as described in the key, and he would thus himself produce the proper sounds of the words without further help from the teacher.

Again, words which offer generally great difficulties in consequence of the strangeness of their orthography, yield as readily to this method as the easier ones, particularly through the use of the " marks." Words like *their, there, which, through, plough, dough, beauty*, we represent the(i)r, ther(e), w(h)ich, thrō(ugh), plou(gh), do(ugh) b(ea)ūty. From the picture of each word as represented here, a child acquainted with the signs can produce the proper sound of each word with the greatest ease.

On the *close connection* of *Writing with Reading* a few words may be necessary.

In the first instance it ought to seem the most natural course that if children have to learn both *reading and writing*, they should not only learn them together, but also the former through the latter, as every word before it can be read must either have been written or printed. And if it cannot be denied that when these two sister arts are separately taught, it frequently happens that children have great difficulties in effecting their connection, it may, *prima facie*, be expected that some advantage will be gained in teaching them simultaneously, the one through the other. Experience has proved that this is really the case.

But there is a further advantage in favour of teaching reading through writing. It has already been shown that the *sound pictures* as produced by spelling the words are distorted representations; whereas the picture of each word as written *phonically* or its *graphic picture* is always correct. Why should we not utilize this radical difference and convey our first instruction through the *eye* rather by means of well defined and correct symbols than by the *ear* by means of unintelligible and misleading *sound pictures*. And here, again, the " marks " render good service.

Difficult words being, so to say, *more marked*, make a deeper impression upon the mind of the young than the easier ones, and are thus brought almost on a level with the latter.

It is, however, not necessary for the children to copy the " marks " when they copy the words.

Those not at all acquainted with the art of teaching reading, as well as those teachers who think that the highest wisdom in teaching consists in going steadily along an old, well-trodden path of routine, will with difficulty be persuaded that so venerable a method, and one so generally followed as the spelling or alphabetic method is radically wrong and injurious. They know so well, and consider it so natural, that the letters w-h-i-c-h represent the word *which;* but to children this, as at present pronounced, is a mystery, as great as that a £5 note should represent five sovereigns, *unless they are* TOLD. And in that really all the difference lies. We wish children with their own eyes and with their own intellect to see what they have to learn, and not to make them the passive instruments of their teachers. Besides, we wish to give them while young the pure gold, and make them acquainted with our conventional contrivances when they are old enough to understand them, and also old enough not to be intellectually injured by them.

The most natural course in affixing the "marks" to letters having various sounds, appeared to the Author to examine which sound, on any page, occurred most frequently; or which was the *prevailing* sound of each of those letters, and he allowed then the usual letter to stand for that sound, whilst its *varieties*, occurring less frequently, received the "marks."

The *prevailing* sound, for instance, of *a* is that in *man*, and *far ;* the *varieties* which we have are the a in *fare* and that in *war*, and are represented by ā and ạ respectively.

The prevailing sound of *i* is not I, the pronoun, but *i* as it sounds in *will, inn, which.* In the Lord's Prayer, for instance, the letter *i* occurs twenty times, and in only *one* of them it has the *I* sound represented ī ; whereas sixteen sound like *i* as in *which, in, kingdom,* &c.

Similarly, the hard sound of *c*, as in *cat*, is the *prevailing* sound; its variety, as in *mice*, is represented ç.

The following additional remarks are given to enable any teacher previously unacquainted with this method to avail himself of it. Before this little book is placed in the hands of the pupils, the following excercises are recommended :—

I. *Preparatory Exercises for the Eye and Hand.*

1. Comparison of dots in various positions on the black board to secure that the children have accurate notions of what is meant by "above," "below," "right," "left," &c. Also drawing lines on the board by the teacher to explain such notions as a "straight line" (for horizontal), "upright" (for perpendicular), "slanting," "slanting to the right," "slanting up," "round," "crooked," "half," "quarter," "thick," "thin," &c.

2. Drawing these lines by the pupils on their slates, first with the help of a ruler, a book, or a slip of paper ; afterwards, freehand.

The order suggested to be followed is indicated at the commencement of the "Introductory Exercises." Parallel with the above must be practised the—

## II. *Preparatory Exercises for the organs of Speech.*

1. Exercises in *Speaking* and *Pronunciation*, for which object lessons, such as are briefly sketched in the "Easy Reading Lessons," page 56, &c., afford materials.

The object of these exercises is to strengthen the children's organs of speech, to accustom them to a correct pronunciation, and to make them think.

2. Analysis of a piece of poetry *into words, syllables*, and *sounds*.

The pupils should commit to memory the first stanza of the subjoined piece of poetry, the teacher saying line after line slowly and distinctly, and the pupils repeating after him, both in chorus and singly.

Then the teacher should say it again line after line, stopping after every word, the children counting how often he stops, thus *learning* of how many words each line and stanza consists.

They should then say in turn, "Oh" is a word, "I" is a word, "Love" is a word, &c. So with each of the three stanzas. To effect the analysis of the words into *syllables*, the teacher would let the children find out that words, for the utterance of which we have to make only *one* effort, like "Oh," "I," "love," "the," &c., consist of *one* syllable; while those for the utterance of which we have to make two, three, or more efforts, like, "mer-ry," "sun-shine," "ho-li-day," consist of *two, three*, or more syllables. As in the analysis of the lines into words, the pupils, one after the other, will say of how many syllables each word consists. Lastly, the syllables are resolved into *sounds*. The teacher again, in the first instance, would pronounce slowly and distinctly a syllable consisting of more than one sound, l-o-ve, when the pupils will have no difficulty in discovering that the word "love" consists of *three sounds*, l-o-ve; the syllable "mer," of the three, "m-e-r;" ry of two, r-y; "sun" of three, s-u-n; "shine" of three, sh-i-ne; "it" of two, i-t; "makes" of four, m-a-ke-s, &c., and so on with every word. In this manner the whole piece of poetry will be analysed into *words, syllables,* and *sounds*. We subjoin the complete analysis into *words, syllables,* and *sounds*, of the piece of poetry. That into words being self-evident, the lines marked (1) indicate the *syllables*, and the lines (2) show the *sounds*.

(1)—Oh, I love the mer-ry sun-shine!
(2)—O, I l-o-v(e) th-e m-e-r-r-y s-u-n-sh-i-n(e)!
(1)—It makes my heart so gay,
(2)—I-t m-a-k-(e)s m-y h-ea-r-t s-o g-ay,
(1)—To hear the sweet birds sing-ing
(2)—T-o h-ea-r th-e s-w-ee-t b-i-r-d-s s-i-ng-i-ng
(1)—On their sum-mer ho-li-day.
(2)—O-n th-ei-r s-u-m-m-e-r h-o-l-i-d-ay.

(1)—Oh, I love the mer-ry sun-shine!
(2)—O, I l-o-v(e) th-e m-e-r-r-y s-u-n-sh-i-n(e)!
(1)—The dew-y mor-ning hour;
(2)—Th-e d-ew-y m-o-r-n-i-ng (h)ou-r;
(1)—With ro-sy smiles ad-van-cing,
(2)—W-i-th r-o-s-y s-m-i-l-(e)s a-d-v-a-n-c-i-ng,
(1)—Like a beau-ty from her bow-er.
(2)—L-i-k(e) a b-eau-t-y f-r-o-m h-e-r b-ow-e-r.

(1)—Oh, it charms the soul from sad-ness,
(2)—O, i-t ch-a-r-m-s th-e s-ou-l f-r-o-m s-a-d-n-e-ss,
(1)—It sets the spi-rit free ;
(2)—I-t s-e-t-s th-e s-p-i-r-i-t f-r-ee ;
(1)—The sun-shine is all beau-ty,
(2)—Th-e s-u-n-sh-i-n(e) i-s a-ll b-eau-t-y,
(1)—Oh, the mer-ry sun for me.
(2)—O, th-e m-e-r-r-y s-u-n f-o-r m-e.

Teachers not experienced in analysing words into sounds, and who may be diffident in performing the operation with other words, will notice that it really consists in nothing but pronouncing each word so slowly as to render its constituent sounds discernible by detaching the one from the other. And this slow pronunciation is the key, so to say, of the constituent sounds of each word, and can be applied readily by any teacher after a little practice.

The shorter or longer practice of the "Preparatory Exercises," depending entirely upon the degree of mental development of the children to be taught, must be left to the judgment of the teacher, who might even dispense with them almost entirely in teaching a small class of intelligent children. With large classes they have the invaluable advantage of preparing all the pupils so as to secure with most of them rapid progress in the main objects:—

## III. Reading and Writing.

In introducing these, the teacher will write on the black board the letter *o*, the pupils copy it, and call it *o*. Then the letter *n* is written on the board, called *n*, not *enn*, and again copied by the children. Then the combinations of these letters *on* and *no* are written on the board, and are read and copied by the children.

After they have thus learned the first lesson in reading and writing *from the board*, then only the little book should be placed in their hands, and they will go over the same lesson again from the book. In a similar manner every other lesson must be treated, following closely the course of the book. It is, however, not necessary for the children to write the *whole of the longer lessons* the first time the course is gone through; the part marked (*a*) only of these lessons may prove sufficient. The rest, marked (*b*), may be written by them when the course is gone through for the second or third time.

From the plan of the work it will be clear that the beginner has only to deal with *one kind of letters* both for *writing and reading*. This has the advantage of avoiding confusion; and until a child has perceived that reading is the easiest and most natural process of the world, nothing ought to be introduced which might prove a stumbling block to him. But it must be left to each teacher to decide whether to postpone the reading of the *second part*, which contains the materials of the first in letter-press characters, until the first is completed, or until the child is about half-way through the first. The rest of the method is sufficiently indicated in the book at the various stages. Children who have mastered this little book can continue their studies by reading any good elementary reading book, by copying, writing from dictation, spelling, &c.

On no account should the pupils be hurried on to the next lesson before they have completely mastered the preceding one. It is also of the utmost importance that the teacher should require his pupils, at an early stage, to connect the sounds of each word one with another, and not to stop after each. They must pronounce in one flow of voice, for instance, the word "wall" just as the letters are connected in writing; and it must be as little permitted to the pupils to read w-a-ll as he would be allowed to write it in that fashion.

As a matter of course the indication of the sounds of the letters before the lessons in the text, as well as the key, are not intended for the pupils, but for the teachers; the key serving only as a kind of index to the sounds, the pupils learn them gradually as they are introduced in the lessons.

Teaching elementary reading and writing is generally considered tedious work to teachers and pupils. Experience has proved that if these most important subjects are treated by the method recommended, and made available by the author, the task of the teachers will be greatly lessened, and the pupils will find amusement and pleasure in their first studies, while, at the same time, their intellect is expanded under the very process of laying the foundation, and of acquiring the most important key to their future studies.

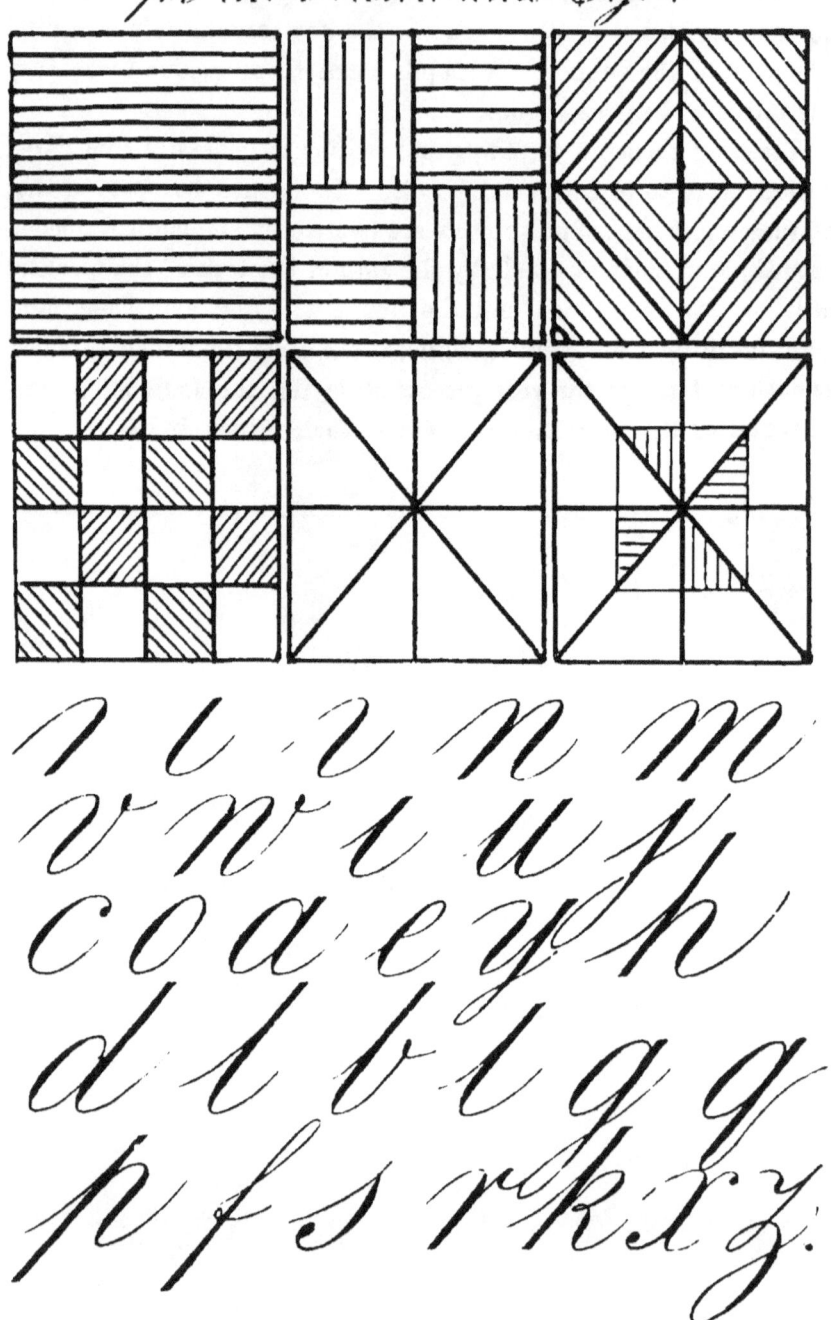

## 1st Part.

o - o in so.

1. o n on no.

---

a - a in man and - a in far.

2. a an na nan.

---

3. m om am mo
ma man mam - ma

---

i - i in pin.

4. i in im ni mi nim min.

---

ā - a in fate.

5.(a.) l ol al il lo la li nol mal nil mil.

(b) lo, ā man in ā mill.

e - e in bed ; ē - e in be.
6(a) e en em el ne mē le
tē men nel mēam mē(a)l.
(b) men in an inn.

u - u in nun.
7. u un um ul nu mu
lu nun num lum
nul lull mull.

8(a) s os as is es so sa si
se sēē sē(a) son sam
sill sell sum miss
less miss lass nos.

3

men sēē sam on ā sill.
is moss in ā sēa? no.
_____

9(a) r ' or ar ir er ur ro ra
ri re rē ru roll ran
rim rum nor more)
mōre) are) māre) sore) rose).
(b) sell mē some) moss or ā
rose).
_____

ō - o in to.
10(a) tot at it et ut to ta ti
te tu not lot lit let mat
sat nut tom tell tin ten
tēa) toss tun tore) tar tan

4.

lāte,) lātę, māt(e); mut-ton
(b) mēat is no mēan mēat.
sit not on a mat.
ten men sat on a tun.
tell tom not to bē too late.)

———

ū- i in like.
11. oō a ā i ū, e ē u n m t s
  r t f.
(a) f, of, af, if, ef, uf, fo, fa, fu
fē, fu, nof, mof, raf, lif,
neff, tuff, for, fot, far, fin,
fine) fell fun fuss fat.
(b) run not too far. a fine)
māre) fell on moss. tea) is
for mam-ma, a nut for mē.

———

c - c in can; c̱ - c in ice.

12(a) c oc uc ic ec nc eo ca c̱i
c̱e cu col cat car can col cof
cāsc; comic; īc̱c; cānc; lac̱c
fāc̱e rāc̱e c̄ɑɟse mīc̱e; cell;
col-lar' cof-fer cof-fēē· mīc̱e;
(b) comc; tō sēē ā· mīc̱c; cāsc;
cof-fēē is in ā· can.
ā· cat can eat mīc̱e.

———

a - a in ball;
ū - u in bull and - u in use.

13(a) b ob ab ib eb ub bo ba bi
bī be bu ban bill bell būll
nob mob rub fob cab bat

bun ball bone bāre beār
boōl robe; but-ler ban-ner
(b) ā fat bull can not run
far; bēef is nice tō ēat;
ā bat is for tom, a ball
for mē.

———

14(a) d od ad id īd ed ud
do dō da dī dū doll dāte
dol den dāme dull lad
led lēad red cod bad bid
fāde bud sūde sad sāid
(b) sam is not ā bad lad.
do not bē so dull; it is of
no ūse. ro-ses are red.

o ō a ā ą i ū I e ē w ū n
m l s r t f c c̱ b d h.
15.(a) h ch ah ch ho ha hū
hē has hill ham her
half hē(a)r hot hose hen
hol hūre hēre hut hoe
(b) lēad me tō ā hut; it is
on ā hill; nē(a)r hēre:
ten men sat in ā hall
and ate some mut-ton.
___

g - g in go; ḡ - g in gem.
16.(a) g og ag ig eg ug go
ga gi gi ge dog nag leg
gar bag dig big fag tug

log gall get got gāt(e) gōōs(e)
gem āge cāge rāge sāge
(h)uge gin gar-den gin-ger.
(b) Sam had a big dog;
it ran af-ter a hare.
his sis-ter has lace and
a fine gem; her age is
not great; but min(e) is less.

———

17(a) p ip ap ip ep up
pe pa pē pē pu nap
map lip sap pin pen
pit peg pig fop pule
pale put top pie rope
so(a)p pope pace pi(e)ce

peace page, pa-pa pā per.
(b) get mē ā pin tō put
in tō his tie.

pa-pa got mē ā nīc(e)
pet-dog, it is so nēat.

18(a) v ov av iv īv ev ēv
uv vo va vi vī ve vē vu.
van vat lov(e) hāv(e) liv(e)
life giv(e) vīce voice fīv(e)
dov(e) mōv(e) siev(e) lēav(e.
(b) five men sat on ā vat.
I hāve ā dove, it can live
on rīce. an ov-en is hot.
give mē ā pen and ā map,
and lēave mē ā-lone.

ou and ow – ou in house.
19.(a) w–v, V o(u) n(u) a(w) wo(e).
wa wi we wet web wig
was who what whip write
wood would were where
cow bow bow now rout
row owl fowl win-ter
win-ner wa-ter wo-man.
(b) Now I will not go
out, for it is wet. we had
no awl and no saw in
our house. a high wall
was built on a low hill.
a cow has two horns.
———

ew - w in use.

20. o o O a ā ạ i ū I e c̄ u ū
ou ow ạw n m l s S r t
f c c̱ C b d h g g̣ p v w k ck.
(a) k ck ok(e) ock āk(e) uck
īke ick ēk(e) eck ūke uck
kā kē ki poke rock cāke
sack like sick wēak week
deck dūke luck māk(e)
kāt(e) kit(e) book look kiss
wick (k)nif(e) (k)no(w) (k)nigh
new few dew pew right.
b.) māke a nice cāke for kāte,
where is a (k)nife to cut it.

I (know) Clare has a new book, it looks well. I have a kite. we do not like wine but milk.

---

21 (a) th Th A-a; tho tha thī thē thu oth ath ith eth uth thin then than thēē that this those these thus there their with lath lāthe pith death path Seth mo-ther fa-ther le(a)-ther.

(b) This path will lēad to thē rock; is it steep?

Seth please take me there. I would, but I have no time. That lath is thin, it will break.

A daughter loves her father and mother.

Their friends often call on them.

---

22(a) sh osh ash ish esh ush sho sha shi she shu nash mash mesh dash sash rash fish push ship shut bush rush

shine, shock shall should
wish hush sun-shine.
(b) I shall not rush
in to the bush.
Our maid has broken
the dish, she has a red sash.
The fine ship will
dash a-gainst the rock.

23 (a) j J jo jā ji je ju
jot jet Jim John jut
Jane jog Job jar
wāge cāge rāge.
(b) Jane, get me a jug of
milk and the jar with jam.

The par-rot in its cage got in-to a rage.

---

24 (a) x X or ax ix ex ux box axe) wax vex mix six fix sex tax fox lax ox-en ex-pense.
(b) please give me six pence, to get a box. The axe, saw, plane and ham-mer are used to build a house. The ox would kick Sam if he were to vex him.

y Y - y in yes and in very
y - y in thy.

25. O o a ā a A I ī x ē
u ū U ou ow aw ew n
m l s T r t T f c c C
b d h g g p v V w k
ck th Th sh Sh j J x.
(a) y Y. yo yē you
yon yes yet yell by ty
ny my dy ly by thy
dye why buy shy rye
boy buy sy ma-ny ve-ry
luc-ky six-ty man-ly mer-
-ry bad-ly tru-ly sad-ly they
key say day.

(6) You should learn your les-son ve-ry well. ma-ny boys have fine toys. I will buy a nice doll for our ba-by. wash your hands and face. Can you read and write a let-ter?

q Q qu — cw or kw —

26(a) L-l Quo qua qui que quoth quaff quack quill quit quick quell quash Queen queer quite qui-et li-quid.

(b) Let us run quick-ly to see the Queen.

This quiet man is not a quack, but he has a queer look. You are right. I hope your mother is quite well. Yes Sir, thank you.

---

27 (a) z З oz az iz ez uz zo za zi ze zu buzz quiz fizz size teaze prize breeze.

(b) Victor should not teaze the kitten. You will receive a book of good size as a prize, if you study with zeal.

---

ch, tch – ch in church;
dge – dge in lodge.

28(a.) G – g, ch, tch dge
tch utch itch etch utch
odge udge idge edge udge
rich much such notch
lodge ditch fetch hatch
latch badge judge ridge
budge ledge which
church ache Christ
chair Charles yacht.

b.) The rich merchant
does not keep his money
in his lodge, but in a

safe in the bank. Charles be quick and fetch my latch-ke(y) from my draw(-ers.

ng = ny in sing;
au, ow = a; ugh = ff
tion = shon; ph = f.

29(a) N=n M=m H=h

nang sing wing
song tongue bring fling
thing think bank ought
naught brought fought
thought caught taught

sought bough, plough,
dough, cough rough,
e-nough, though, through,
tho-rough, bo-rough,
por-tion cau-tion lo-tion
mo-tion phi-al pro-phet
child chil-dren lit-tle
ap-ple ta-ble word world
stick staff snow snail
aunt bro-ther sis-ter.
(b) Hugh's cau-tion
dur-ing play is great.

he is not rough but merry. The little bird which is sitting on a high tree, is singing during a portion of the day. do not leave the carriage while the train is in motion, you might fall and be killed.

30. 1. Oh, I love the merry sun-shine; It makes my heart so gay

To hear the sweet birds
sing-ing,
On their sum-mer ho-
li-day.
———

2. Oh I love the mer-ry
sun-shine,
The dew-y morn-ing
hour,
With ro-sy smiles ad-
vanc-ing
Like a beau-ty from
her bow-er.
———

3. Oh, it charms the soul from sad-ness, It sets the spi-rit free; The sun-shine is all beau-ty, Oh, the mer-ry sun for me!

---

6. The Lord's Prayer.

---

Our Fa-ther which art in heav-en, Hal-low-ed be thy name. Thy king-dom come. Thy will be done in earth, as it is in heav-en. Give us this day our daily bread. And for-give us our tres-pass-es as we for-give them that tres-pass against us. And lead us not in-to temp-ta-tion; but de-liver us from evil: for thine is the king-dom, and the pow-er and the glo-ry, for ev-er and ev-er. A-men.

31(a) o ŏ a ā ȧ i ī ė ē u ū
O A I E U

n m l s r t
N M L S R T

f c c̱ b d h
F C B D H

g ḡ p r̆ w k
G P V W K

j x̆ y q z
J X Y Q Z

(b) one 1, two 2,
three 3, four 4,
five 5, six 6,

sev-en 7,     eight 8,
nine 9,       ten 10,
e-lev-en 11,  twelve 12,
twen-ty 20,   thir-ty 30,
for-ty 40,    hun-dred 100,
thou-sand 1000,
Sun-day   Mon-day
Tues-day  Wed-nes-day
Thurs-day  Fri-day
Sa-tur-day.

32. Ann, A-dam, A-si-a,
Ben, Bet-sy, Bri-tain,
Clare, Charles, Cam-bridge,

Do-ra, Da-vid, Do-ver,
Eve, Ed-ward, Eng-land,
Frank, Flo-ra, Folk-stone,
George, Ger-trude, Green-wich,
Hel-en, Hen-ry, Har-wich,
I-da, Is-aac, Ire-land,
Jane, James, Ja-mai-ca,
Kate, Kent, Kings-ton,
Lil-ly, Lew-is, Lon-don,
Ma-ry, Mo-ses, Mal-ta,
Nan-cy, Nep-tune, Nor-folk,
Ot-to, Ol-ive, O-der,

Paul, Phæ-be, Pa-ris,
Que-bec, Queens-town,
Rose, Ro-bert, Rich-mond,
Sā-rah, Ste-phen, Se-vern,
Thē-o-dore, Thames,
Ur-ban, Ur-sa-la, Up-ton,
Vic-to-ri-a, Ve-nice,
Win-nie, Wil-li-am, Wales,
Xer-xes, Xer-es,
York, York-shire,
Ze-cha-rī-ah, Zu-rich.

## Key.

a - a in man, and - a in far.
ā - a in fate; ą - a in ball.
e - e in bed; ē - e in be.
i - i in pin and in bird;
ī - i in like.
o - o in on, so; ō - o in to.
u - u in nun.
ū - u in full and u in use.
y - y in yes; ȳ - y in thy.
ou and ow = ou in house.
au, aw and oụ = ą; ew - ū.
c - c in can; ҫ = c in ice.

g - g in go; ḡ = g in gem.
ch tch = ch in church.
dge - dge in lodge.
sh - sh in she.
th - th in that and these.
qu - cw or kw - quick.
ng - ng in sing.
tion - shon, - portion.
ph - f - phial.
ugh - ff - rough.

 A letter or letters that are not sounded are put in brackets:

 se(a), tho(ugh).

# SECOND PART.   SECTION A.

o  n  a  m  i  l  u  s  r.

*o  n  a  m  i  l  u  s  r.*

o = o in so.

1—o  n  on  nō.

a = a in man and = a in far.

2—a  an  na  nan.

3—m  om  am  mo  ma  man  mam-ma.

i = i in pin.

4—i  in  im  ni  mi  nim  min.

ā = a in fate.

5(*a*)—l ol al il lo la li nol mal nil mil.

(*b*)—lo ā man in ā mill.

---

e = e in bed ; ē = e in be.

6(*a*)—e en em el ne mē le lē men nel mē(a)n mē(a)l.

(*b*)—men in an inn.

---

u = u in nun.

7—u un um ul nu mu lu nun num lum nul lull.

---

8(*a*)—s os as is es so sa si se sēē sē(a) son sam sill sell sum miss less moss lass nos.

(*b*)—men sēē sam on ā sill.
is moss in ā sē(a) ? no.

---

9(*a*)—r or ar ir er ur ro ra ri re rē
ru roll ran rim rum nor mor(e)
mēr(e) ar(e) mār(e) sor(ē) rōs̱(e).

(*b*)—sell mē som(e) moss or ā rōs̱(e).

t   f   c   b   d   n   g   I   S

*t   f   c   b   d   h   g   I   S*

---

ŏ = o in to.

10(*a*)—t ot at it et ut to ta ti te tu
not lot lit let mat sat nut

tom tell tin ten te(a) toss tun
tor(e) tar tan tāl(e) lāt(e)
māt(e) ; mutton.

(b)—mē(at) is no mē(a)n mē(a)l.
sit not on a mat.
ten men sat on ā tun.
tell tom not tō bē tōō lāt(e).

---

i = i in like.

11—o ō a ā i ī e ē u n m l s r t f.

(a)—f of af if ef uf fo fa fī fē fu
nof mof raf lif neff tuff for fol
far fin fīn(e) fell fun fuss fat.

(a)—run not tōō far. ā fīn(e)
mār(e) fell on moss. tē(a)
is for mam-ma, ā nut for me,

c = c in can; c̬ = c in ice.

**12(a)**—c oc ac ic ec uc co ca c̬i c̬e
cu cot cat car can col cof
cās(e) com(e) īc̬(e) cān(e) lāc̬e
fāce rac̬e cē(a)se mīc̬(e) c̬ell;
collar cof-fēē nīc̬(e).

(b)—com(e) to sēē a nīc̬e cās(e).
cof-fēē is in ạ can.
ạ cat can ē(a)t mīc̬e.

---

a = a in ball;
u̇ = u in bull and = u in use.

**13(a)**—b ob ab ib eb ub bo ba bi
bī be bu ban bill bell bu̇ll
nob mob rub fob cab bat bun
ball bon(e) bar(e) b(e)ār bōōt
rob(e); but-ter ban-ner.

(b)—ā fat būll can not run far;
bēēf is nīce tō ē(a)t.

---

14(a)—d od ad id īd ed ud do dō
da dī dū doll dāt(e) dot den
dām(e) dull lad led lē(a)d red
cod bad bid făd(e) bud sīd(e)
sad sā(i)d.

(b)—sam is not ā bad lad. Dō not
bē so dull, it is of no ūs(e).
ro-ses ar(e) red.

---

o ō a ă a̱ i ī I e ē u ū n m l s r t f c c̱
b d h.

15(a)—h oh ah eh ho ha hī hē has
hill ham her ha(l)f hear hot

hos(e) hen hot hār(e) hēr(e) hut hoc.

(*b*)—lē(a)d mē tō ā hut; it is on ā hill, nē(a)r hēr(e). Ten men sat in ā hall and āte som(e) mut-ton.

---

g = g in go; ḡ = g in gem.

16(*a*)—g og ag ig eg go ga gi ḡi ḡe dog nag leg gar bag dig big fag tug log gall get got gāt(e) gōōs(e) ḡem āḡe rāḡe sāḡe (h)ūḡe ḡin gar-den ḡin-ḡer.

(*b*(—Sam had ā big dog, it ran af-ter ā hāre. His sis-ter has

lāce and a̱ fīne ḡem; her āḡe
is not greāt, but mīne is less.

---

p  v  w  k  j  x  y  q  z

*p  v  w  k  j  x  y  q  z*

17(*a*)—p op ap ip ep up po pa pī
pē pū nap map lip sap pin
pen pit peg pig fop pīle pāle
pūt top pīe rope so(a)p pope
pāce p(i)ēce pē(a)ce pāḡe,
pa-pa pā-per.

(*b*)—get mē a̱ pin tō put in-tō
his tīe. Pa-pa got mē a̱
nīc(e) pet-dog, it is so nē(a)t.

18(a)—v ov av iv īv ev ēv uv vo va vi vī ve vē vu van vat lov(e) hāv(e) liv(e) līf(e) giv(e) vīc(e) fīv(e) dov(e) mōv(e) si(e)v(e) lē(a)ve.

(b)—fīve men sat on ā vat. I hāve ā dove, it can live on rīce. An oven is hot. Give mē ā pen and ā map, and lē(a)ve mē ā-lone.

---

V O C T A J X Y

*V O C T A J X Y*

ou and ow = ou in house.

19(a)—w v, Vow o(w) a(w) wo(e) wa wī wē wet web wig was (w)hō

w(h)at w(h)ip wōōd wŏ(ul)d
were w(h)er(e) cow how bo(w)
now rout ro(w) owl fowl;
win-ter win-ner wa-ter wŏ-man

(*b*)—I will not go out, for it is wet.
we had no a(w)l and no sa(w)
in our hous(e). A hī(gh) wall
was (bu)ilt on a lo(w) hill. A
cow has t(w)ō horns.

---

ew = ū in use.

20—o ō O a ä a i ī I e ē u ū ou ow
a(w)n m l s S r t f c c C b d h g
ḡ p v w k ck.

(*a*)—k ck ok(e) ock āk(e) ack īk(e)
ick ēk(e) eck ūk(e) uck kā kē

kī poke rock cāke sack līke
sick wē(a)k wĕĕk deck dūk(e)
luck māk(e) kāt(e) kīt(e) bōōk
lōōk wick kiss (k)nīf(e) (k)no(w)
(k)nī(gh)t new few dew pew.

(*b*)—māke a nīce cāke for kāte;
w(h)ere is a (k)nīfe tō cut it?
I know Clār(e) has a new bōōk,
it looks well. I have a kīt(e).
wē dō not līke wīne but milk.

---

21 (*a*)—th Th A a; tho tha thī thē thu
oth ath ith eth uth thin then
than thēē that this those thēse
thus there the(i)r with lath
lāthe pith de(a)th path Seth

mother fa-ther le(a)-ther.

(b)—This path will le(a)d to the rock. Is it steep? Seth please take me there. I wō(ul)d, but I have no time. That lath is thin; it will breāk. A da(ugh)-ter loves her fa-ther and her mo-ther. The(i)r fr(i)ends of-(t)en call on them.

---

22(a)—sh osh ash ish esh ush sho sha. Shī she shū nash mash mesh dash sash rash fish pūsh ship shut būsh rush shō(e) shock shall shō(u)d wish hush sun-shīne.

(b)—I shall not rush in-to thē būsh.
Our mā(i)d has bro-ken the dish; she has a red sash. Thē fīne ship will dash a-gā(i)nst thē rock.

---

23(a)—j J jo ja jā ji je ju jot jet Jim Jo(h)n jut Jāne jog Job jar wāḡe cāḡe rāḡe.

(b)—Jāne get mē a jug of milk and thē jar with jam. Thē par-rot in its cāḡe got in-to a rāḡe.

---

24(a)—x X ox ax ix ex ux box ax(e) wax vex mix six fix sex tax fox lax ox-en ex-pense.

(b)—Plē(a)se give mē six penc(e) to get ā box. Thē axe, sa(w), plāne, and ham-mer are ūs(e)d to b(u)ild a house. Thē ox wō(ul)d kick Sam if he were tō vex him

---

y, Y ; = y in yes and in very ; ȳ = y in thȳ.

25—O ō a ā a̤ A l i ī e ē u ū.  U ew ow a(w) ew n m l s S r t T f c c̣ C b d h g ḡ p v V w k ck th Th sh Sh j J x.

(a)—y Y. yo yē y(o)ū yon yes yet yell by ty ny my dy ly by thy dye w(h)y b(u)y shy rye boy bu-sy ma-ny ve-ry luc-ky six-ty man-ly mer-ry bad-ly trū-ly sad-ly the(y) hĕ(y) sā(y) dā(y).

(b)—Yō(u) shō(ul)d le(a)rn yō(u)r les-son ve-ry well. Ma-ny boys have fīne toys. I will b(u)y a a nīce doll for our ba-by. Wash yōūr hands and fāce. Can yōū rē(a)d and (w)rīte a let-ter?

Q L Z G N M H W

*Q L Z G N M H W*

q Q qu = cw or kw. L = l.

26(a)—Qui qua qui que quoth quaff quack quill quit quick quell quash Queen queer quite qui-et li-quid.

(b(—Let us run quick-ly tō sēē thē Queēn. This quī-et man is not a quack, but hē has a queer lōōk. You are rī(gh)t. I hope yō(u)r mo-ther is quīte well. Yes, Sir, thank yō(u).

---

27(a)—z Z oz az iz ez uz zo za zi ze zu buzz quiz fizz sīze tē(a)ze prīze brēēze.

(b)—Victor shō(ul)d not tē(a)zē the kit-ten. You will re-cē(i)ve a book of good sīze as a prīze, if you stu-dy with zeal.

ch tch = ch in church; dge = dge in lodge.

28(a)—G = g, ch tch dge otch atch etch utch odge adge idge edge udge rich much such notch lodge ditch fetch hatch latch badge judge ridge budge ledge w(h)ich church āc(he) C(h)rīst chā(i)r Charl(e)s ya(ch)t

(b)—The rich mer-chant do(e)s not keep his mo-ney in his lodge, but in a safe in the bank. Charles be quick and fetch my latch kē(y) from my dra(w)ers.

---

ng = ng in sing; au, ou = a, ugh = ff; tion = shon; ph = f.

29(a)—N = M  m = H  h  nang  sing

wing song tong(ue) bring fling
thing think bank ou(gh)t
nau(gh)t brou(g)ht fou(gh)t
thou(g)ht cau(g)ht tau(gh)t
sou(gh)t bou(gh) plou(gh)
dou(gh) cough rough ē-nough
tho(ugh) thrō(ugh) tho-ro(ugh)
bo-ro(ugh) por-tion cau-tion
lo-tion mo-tion phī-al pro-phet
child child-ren lit-tle ap-ple
ta-ble word world stick staff
snow snā(i)l a(u)nt bro-ther.

(b)—Hū(gh)'s cau-tion dūr-ing play is great, he is not rough but mer-ry. The lit-tle bird, w(h)ich is sit-ting on a hī(gh) trēē, is sing-ing dūr-ing a por-tion of the dā(y). Do not lē(a)ve the car-ri(a)ge whīle the trā(i)n is in mo-tion, yōū mī(ght) fall and be kil-l(e)d.

---

30(1)—Oh, I love the mer-ry sun-shīne,
It māūes my h(e)art so gāy;
To hear the swēēt birds sing-ing
On the(i)r sum-mer ho-li-dāy.

---

(2)—Oh, I love the mer-ry sun-shine;
The dew-y morn-ing hour,
With rosy smīl(e)s ad-van-cing,
Like a b(ea)ū-ty from her bower.

(3)—Oh, it c̬harms the so(u)l from sad-ness,
It sets the spi-rit frēē ;
The s̬un-shine is all b(ea)ū̇-ty;
Oh, the mer-ry sun for me.

---

## THE LORD'S PRAYER.

(*b*)—O̬ur Fa-ther which art in heav-en. Hal-low-ed be thy name. Thy king-dom come. Thy will be done in earth, as it is in heav-en. Give us this day our dai-ly bread. And for-give us our tres-pass-es as we for-give them that tres-pass against us. And lead us not in-to temp-ta-tion, but de-liv-er us from e-vil; for thine is the king-dom, and the pow-er and the glo-ry for ev-er and ev-er. A-men.

---

31 (a)—o ō  a ā a̤  i ī  e ē  u ū

| O | A | I | E | U |
|---|---|---|---|---|

| n | m | l | s | r | t |
|---|---|---|---|---|---|
| N | M | L | S | R | T |

| f | c | c̱ | b | d | h | g |
|---|---|---|---|---|---|---|
| F | C | B | D | H | G |

| p | v | w | k | j | x |
|---|---|---|---|---|---|
| P | V | W | K | J | X |

| x | y | q | z |
|---|---|---|---|
| X | Y | Q | Z |

(b)—one 1, t(w)o 2, thrēē 3, four 4, fīve 5, six 6, sev-en 7, e(igh)t 8, nīne 9, ten 10, e-lev-en 11, twelve 12, twen-ty 20, thir-ty 30, for-ty 40, hun-dred 100, thou-sand 1000.

Sun-dāy  Mondāy  Tū(e)sdāy
We(d)-n(e)s-dāy   Thurs-dāy
Frī-dāy Sa-tur-dāy.

---

32—Ann      A-dam      A-si-a
   Ben       Bet-sy     Bri-tain
   Clāre     Charles    Cam-bridge
   Do-ra     Da-vid     Do-ver
   Eve       Ed-ward    Eng-land
   Frank     Flo-ra     Fo(l)k-stone
   G(e)orge  Ger-trude  Green-(w)ich

| | | |
|---|---|---|
| Hel-en | Hen-ry | Har-(w)ich |
| I-da | Is-aac | Ire-land |
| Jāne | James | Ja-mā(i)-ca |
| Kāte | Kent | Kings-ton |
| Lil-ly | Lew-is | Lon-don |
| Mā-ry | Mo-ses | Mal-ta |
| Nan-cy | Nep-tūne | Nor-folk |
| Ot-to | Ol-ive | O-der |
| Pa(u)l | Phœ-be | Pa-ris |
| Que-bec | Queēns-town | |
| Rose | Ro-bert | Rich-mond |
| Sā-rah | Ste-phen | Se-vern |
| Thē-o-dore | | Thames |
| Ur-ban | Ur-sa-la | Up-ton |
| Vic-to-ria | | Ven-ice |
| Win-nie | Wil-li-am | Wāles |
| Xer-xes | | Xer-es |
| Ze-cha-rī-ah | Zu-rich. | |

# SECOND PART. SECTION B.

## EASY READING LESSONS.†

### 1.—BREAD.*

Bread is made of dough, dough of flour, flour of corn. Corn grows in the field. The far-mer sows corn, and God caus-es it to grow by send-ing rain.

### 2.—MILK.

We get milk from the cow ; it is sweet, and chil-dren like to drink it. The rich-est part of milk is called cream. Of cream we make but-ter. But-ter is put up-on bread. We like bread and but-ter  Of what is cheese made ?  Por-ridge is made of milk and flour.

### 3.—MEAT.

Meat we get from the ox, the calf, the pig, the stag, the deer, the fowl, the goose. Men-tion the names of oth-er an-i-mals whose flesh we eat. Meat is whole-some, and gives strength. Child-ren need less meat than grown up peo-ple.

---

† The Easy Reading Lessons, from 1 to 27, are free translations of lessons taken from the "Fibel," or first reading book used in Würt-temberg.

* NOTE.—All these exercises must also first be copied by the pupils, and later written from dictation.

## 4.—Fruit.

Fruit grows on the trees. Do all trees bear fruit? Name one of the trees which bear fruit. When is fruit ripe? Is fruit good to eat if it is not ripe? Ci-der is made from ap-ples. Ci-der is sweet, it is not so strong as wine.

## 5.—The Cher-ry.

The cher-ry is red, and of-ten black. It gets ripe in May. Who likes cher-ries? In the cher-ry is a stone, and in the stone is a ker-nel. Is the ker-nel good to eat?

## 6.—The Pear.

The pear is eat-en fresh; it is also dried for win-ter; per-ry is made of it. It hangs by the stalk on the twig, the twig is on the branch, and the branch on the stem. There is no stone in the pear, what is in it in-stead?

## 7.—The Ber-ry.

The ber-ry grows on a shrub. It looks red, black, yel-low, and brown. There are some ber-ries which we must not eat, they cause pain and death. Be care-ful not to eat a ber-ry, un-less you know that it will not hurt you.

## 8.—The Horse.

The horse is tall, fine, and strong. Its tail is long, and has plen-ty of hair. Some horses kick; there-fore, do not go near them. They can run very quick-ly, and with reins you can guide them, either to the right, or to the left, as you like. The horse is al-so cal-led a steed, charg-er, and cours-er. There are grey, black, white, brown, and cream col-our-ed hor-ses.

## 9.—The Ox.

The ox is not so tall as the horse, yet it is very strong. The ox toss-es with his horns, therefore be-ware of him! The ox eats grass, hay, clo-ver, and straw. A yoke is put on the ox. It draws the wag-gon and the plough, but it can-not run as fast as the horse. We eat its flesh. What is the meat cal-led that we get from the ox?

## 10.—The Cow.

The cow is near-ly as large as the ox, and her skin and hair look like those of the ox. She gives us milk. Some-times she also is put to the plough. The cow eats what the ox eats. What is made of the cow's skin? and who makes it? Is the flesh of the cow eat-en?

---

\* Note.—All these exercises must also first be copied by the pupils, and later written from dictation.

## 11.—The Pig.

The pig is fond of rol-ling in dirt and mud. How does it look then? The flesh of the pig is eat-en. What is it cal-led? When the flesh of the pig is salt-ed and dried, it is cal-led ba-con or ham. Which do you like the best, ba-con or ham? Ba-con is oft-en ea-ten for break-fast. Lard is made from the fat of the pig.

## 12.—The Sheep.

The sheep is a very tame an-i-mal. Its hair is cur-ly, and is cal-led wool. Yarn is made of wool, and cloth made of yarn. Young sheep are cal-led lambs. They are very gen-tle and tame. They do not kick, or bite, or toss you. They will eat bread out of your hand. What is made of the skin of the sheep and of the lambs.

## 13.—The Dog.

The dog is faith-ful. He is o-be-di-ent to his mas-ter. E-ven if his mas-ter beats him, he still re-mains faith-ful to him and pro-tects him a-gainst his e-ne-my. He guards the house at night and keeps off thieves and bur-glars. The hound is ta-ken to the chase. There he scents the stag, the deer, the fox, and what else? Did you ev-er see a dog swim in wa-ter? If you throw a stick in-to the wa-ter, what will the dog do?

## 14.—The Cat.

The cat caus-es the child much fun by its play. But do not trust it, it is false. It scratch-es if it is teaz-ed. The cat is fond of meat, and steals it when it can. It catch-es mice in the house and out of doors and eats them.

## 15.—The Goose.

The goose is said to be stu-pid; but she is ve-ry use-ful to us. We eat its flesh. We get the quill, with which we write, from the goose, and her fea-thers make very soft beds. She lays large eggs, which are good to eat. There-fore, do not des-pise the goose, though she may be stu-pid.

## 16.—The Fowl.

The fowl is of great use to us. Du-ring sum-mer the hen lays an egg al-most ev-e-ry day. Eggs are boil-ed, and eat-en; we al-so fry them. The flesh of a young fowl is ten-der. It may be boil-ed then to get chick-en broth. The hen scratch-es in heaps of sand and rub-bish in search of food. What is the hen fond of? Has she a nest? The cock crows ear-ly in the morn-ing. Did you ev-er hear it and then get up?

## 17.—The Stork.

The stork has long legs. He is stand-ing on the high roof, for there he makes his nest. He flies a-cross the mea-dows and a-bout the swamp; there he looks for food, and takes it to his young ones. Do you know what the stork is fond of? In au-tumn he goes a-way from us far o-ver the land and sea. In March he re-turns and seeks his old nest. Then chil-dren cry out mer-ri-ly, "The Stork has re-turn-ed!"

## 18.—The Dress.

The dress pro-tects the bo-dy a-gainst cold, rain, and wind. It is made of cloth and oth-er ma-te-ri-als, which are wo-ven out of yarn and cot-ton. What is the man cal-led who makes cloth, and what do we call those who make cot-ton goods? Cloth is blue, yel-low, gray, red, white, black, green, brown, and o-ther co-lours. It can be dy-ed just as peo-ple like to have it.

## 19.—The Shirt.

The shirt is made of li-nen or cot-ton. Li-nen is made of flax, and cot-ton of the cot-ton plant. Flax grows in the field; cot-ton is the down of the cot-ton tree, which does not grow in Eng-land, but in warm-er coun-tries. Of flax and cot-ton thread and yarn are spun. Thread and yarn are wo-ven into cloth. How is li-nen made white?

## 20.—The Stock-ing.

The stock-ing is made of yarn. Yarn is spun in the mill. For-mer-ly it was spun by hand. Stock-ings keep the feet warm, and pre-vent them from be-ing rub-bed by the boots and shoes. Girls must learn to mend their stock-ings.

## 21.—The Shoe.

Shoes are made of lea-ther or cloth. Who makes shoes and boots? Boots and shoes pro-tect the foot a-gainst dust, dirt, and wet. Has the horse shoes on his feet also?

## 22.—The Hat.

The hat is a co-ver-ing for the head. It is made of silk, felt, straw, and of what be-sides? What is felt made of? The hat is gen-er-al-ly round; but there are hats which are not round. Has an an-i-mal any cloth-ing? What sort of cloth-ing has the dog, the sheep, the bear, the goose, the frog, the rab-bit?

## 23.—The Table.

The ta-ble stands in the room. The man, the wom-an, the child, eat at the ta-ble. A well be-haved child does not stand, sit, or lie upon the ta-ble; nei-ther does he lay the arm or foot upon it; that would be rude.

## 24.—The Chair.

The chair stands in the room by the wall, and at the ta-ble. It is made of wood, and has four legs, a seat, and a back. Peo-ple sit up-on the chair to eat or drink, and when they are tired. Al-so those who write, paint, or draw sit up-on chairs. Who makes the chairs and ta-bles?

## 25.—The Bench (form).

The bench stands a-gainst the wall. Peo-ple sit up-on it, and some-times they lie up-on it if they are ve-ry tired.

## 26.—The Star-ling.

The old far-mer Jones had in his room a star-ling that could speak a few words. If the far-mer cal-led "Star-ling, where are you?" the star-ling cried, "Here I am." Charles, the son of his neigh-bour, was ve-ry fond of the bird, and oft-en paid the far-mer a visit. Once, when Charles cal-led, the far-mer was not at home. So Charles caught the bird quick-ly, put it into his poc-ket and want-ed to run a-way be-fore the far-mer re-turned, but just then he en-ter-ed the door. He wish-ed to a-muse the boy, and called out, as us-u-al: "Star-ling, where are you?" The bird from the boy's poc-ket cal-led out as loud-ly as he could; "Here I am." Blush-ing for shame, Charles gave up the star-ling, and did not dare to show him-self any more be-fore the far-mer.

### 27.—The Two Goats.

Two goats met on a path that led a-cross a deep tor-rent. One wish-ed to go one way, and the oth-er the op-pos-ite. "Go out of my way," said the one. "You don't mean it," cried the oth-er, "you go back and let me pass; I was first on the ledge." "What do you think," re-plied the first, "I am so much old-er than you, and you ex-pect me to give way to you. No, I shall ne-ver do that." Nei-ther would yield, each want-ed to go first. So they be-gan to fight. They put for-ward their horns and ran a-gainst each oth-er with great force. Through their vio-lent blows they both lost their foot-ing, and fell to-geth-er over the nar-row path in-to the tor-rent.

Be-ware of ob-sti-na-cy.

### 28.—The Dis-o-be-di-ent Lamb.

I will tell you a story a-bout a lamb. There was once a shep-herd, who had a great ma-ny sheep and lambs. He took a great deal of care of them, and gave them sweet fresh grass to eat, and clear wa-ter to drink, and when they were sick he was very good to them; and when they climb-ed up a steep hill, and

# PRIMER

OF

# THE PHONIC METHOD

OF TEACHING

# READING & WRITING SIMULTANEOUSLY

WITH AN

## INTRODUCTION.

BY

G. C. MAST,

*Principal of Belgrave College, Pimlico; author of "French: Practice and Theory"; "Linear Drawing"; &c.*

[*All rights reserved*]

LONDON:
CHARLES BEAN, 81, NEW NORTH ROAD, N.
1875.

PART II

# PREFACE.

A GOOD knowledge of *Reading* and *Writing* is generally admitted to be the foundation of all the other branches of knowledge. But it is not so generally understood that upon the manner in which these fundamental arts of education are acquired by the young, their progress in other studies mainly depends. And yet it might appear reasonable enough to suppose that, as the beginning is, so will be the progress and the final result.

"The results of our existing system of primary education" are pronounced by trustworthy authorities to be "a miserable failure." "Education up to the point of reading and writing to any useful purpose under present circumstances is not attained by the great bulk of the population." "It takes from six to seven years to learn the arts of reading and spelling with a fair degree of intelligence." According to the last Report of the Committee of the

Council of Education, out of a hundred pupils "only nine were presented in the fourth and higher standards."*

The cause of these failures is attributed mainly to the defective alphabet and orthography of the English language. The latter is characterised as "a labyrinth, a chaos, an absurdity, a disgrace to our age,"† and as "a mass of anomalies, the growth of ignorance and chance, equally repugnant to good taste and common sense."‡

What a vicious creature this beautiful English language is represented to be by its friends!

But what if, after all, it should prove to be only a spirited horse, a modern Bucephalus that required nothing more than proper management to be subdued and made willing to obey its leader? Without using whip or spur for guiding it, only by means of bit and bridle, and leading it out of the distorted picture of its own shadow, the Author has succeeded in subduing it, so as to make it subservient to all his wishes.

For years it had been his wish to introduce in this country the *German*, or *Phonic method of teaching reading and writing simultaneously*, not yet, so far as the Author knows, practised in England. But it was not until December last that he had an opportunity of doing so in a lecture which he gave before the College of Pre-

---

\* *Times*, July 1st, 1875.

† Sir C. E. Trevelyan.    ‡ The Bishop of St. David's.

ceptors.* The favourable reception the method he advocated met there encouraged him to submit it to a larger circle of teachers and friends of education in the form of this little book. It contains an adaptation of German principles of teaching reading and writing to the English language. The only novelties in it are the "marks"—strokes, ties, dots, and brackets, to the adoption of which the Author was unintentionally driven; but their utility proved, on trial, greater than could have been anticipated. One example of the capacity of this method may suffice.

A girl not quite six years of age being taught by the Author, could read the first part of this book (in manuscript) after less than three months' instruction; the lessons lasting from 10 to 15 minutes daily.

After six months she could read any easy elementary book; and after nine months, any book within the scope of young children; and at the same time she could read letters, received from her little friends, and answer them.

An elder sister of hers, equally intelligent, but having been taught by the prevailing methods, could not read so fluently after three years' toil as her younger sister after nine months' amusement.

A large class of sixty to eighty children could, by any teacher acquainted with this method, be taught with ease *reading and writing*, intelligently, in less than twelve months.

---

* See *Educational Times*, January, 1875.

Should the exposition of the method in the "Introduction" not prove sufficient, the Author would be happy to explain it further before any School Board, or assembly of teachers.

At the same time he would feel obliged for any suggestion for improvements, addressed to him,

THE AUTHOR.

Belgrave College,
148, Buckingham Palace Road, London.
*September*, 1875.

# INTRODUCTION.

The *uncertainty of the sound* of some letters, and the *anomalies of spelling* in English are the chief obstacles to beginners in reading. And whatever may have been done by compilers of reading books in the way of arranging the words in an easy and systematic manner, no feasible method has been produced which, going to the very root of the evils, has succeeded in overcoming them. The attempts to remove them through the introduction of an altogether new or an enlarged alphabet, or through a remodelling of the spelling of the whole language, must fail on account of the double toil these methods entail of first learning quite a new, and then the usual manner of writing and spelling.

No practical man would erect a large mansion to pull it down again as soon as it is finished, and to build of its materials a smaller house for permanent and ordinary use. But it is a usual thing in building to erect a scaffold to facilitate the operations. And that is what the Author has done. In order to reach the difficulties of the English language he has introduced some external means, called here "Marks." For the removal of difficulties arising from the *uncertainty* of the sound of letters he has affixed *strokes*, *dots* and *ties*, either above or below the letters; and for the removal of those arising from redundancy of letters he has employed the *bracket*. He thus obtained an *ample Phonic alhpabet*, without adding a single new letter, and a *simplified spelling*, without altering the orthography of a single word. As we prepare food for infants, so the English language has been merely *prepared* for the purpose of facilitating the acquisition of the art of reading, and prepared by means which, having served their purpose, can be laid aside as easily as the scaffolding can be taken down when the building is finished, or the leading strings be left off when a child can walk. *English thus prepared* is now in a condition to have principles applied which in Germany are no longer under discussion, but are practised everywhere, underlying every sound method of teaching elementary reading: they consist in *teaching reading phonically and in the closest connection with writing*. In this German method spelling is postponed until a child can read. In teaching reading, instead of the *names* of each consonant only its *phonic value*, power or sound is given; that part, namely, which *sounds together with a vowel in each syllable*, and which we obtain by dropping entirely the *vowel sound of its* name.

The phonic value, for instance, of the letter *b* is obtained by dropping the *ee* of its name; that of *k* by dropping the *ay* of its name, &c. What is left after the dropping of the vowel sound of each consonant is hardly a sound; it becomes one in connection with the vowel of a word or syllable—whence its name *con-sonant* —a letter *sounding with* a vowel. Now, as a means of referring to them the names of the consonants are all necessary; but *spelling* or saying the names of the letters, as a means to teach reading for beginners is not only not necessary, but a grave mistake. For, as a rule, the vowel sounds of the names of the consonants do not tally with those of the words or syllables in which they occur, and must consequently cause confusion in the mind of the young. A few examples will show this clearly. If we take such easy words as *dog, cat, icy,* a child cannot possibly understand that d-o-g, as usually spelt, could sound *dog*; nor c-a-t, cat; nor i-c-y, icy. He will learn the sound of these words not from hearing them spelt, but merely from being told by the teacher, quite mechanically. Far from being pleased to discover a connection between the one and the other, he must be puzzled about the strangeness of this kind of learning; for spelling c-a-t would produce in his mind rather the idea of *see-a-tea*, than *cat*, and spelling i-c-y the idea of *I-see-why* than *icy*. So also o-u-r sounds *oh-you-are*, r-u-n almost *are-you-in ?*, and w-a-x almost *double-you-a-axe ;* worst of all l-a-d might be mistaken for a *lady*.

It is a serious matter thus to disappoint the young with every word they have to spell, but it is a more serious error to expect that children can learn reading easily and intelligently by this method. According to the method proposed, the child would have been taught to pronounce the letters of which *dog, cat, icy, our*, and *run* consist *phonically* and as described in the key, and he would thus himself produce the proper sounds of the words without further help from the teacher.

Again, words which offer generally great difficulties in consequence of the strangeness of their orthography, yield as readily to this method as the easier ones, particularly through the use of the "marks." Words like *their, there, which, through, plough, dough, beauty*, we represent the(i)r, ther(e), w(h)ich, thrō(ugh), plou(gh), do(ugh) b(ea)ūty. From the picture of each word as represented here, a child acquainted with the signs can produce the proper sound of each word with the greatest ease.

On the *close connection* of *Writing with Reading* a few words may be necessary.

In the first instance it ought to seem the most natural course that if children have to learn both *reading and writing*, they should not only learn them together, but also the former through the latter, as every word before it can be read must either have been written or printed. And if it cannot be denied that when these two sister arts are separately taught, it frequently happens that children have great difficulties in effecting their connection, it may, *prima facie*, be expected that some advantage will be gained in teaching them simultaneously, the one through the other. Experience has proved that this is really the case.

But there is a further advantage in favour of teaching reading through writing. It has already been shown that the *sound pictures* as produced by spelling the words are distorted representations; whereas the picture of each word as written *phonically* or its *graphic picture* is always correct. Why should we not utilize this radical difference and convey our first instruction through the *eye* rather by means of well defined and correct symbols than by the *ear* by means of unintelligible and misleading *sound pictures*. And here, again, the " marks " render good service.

Difficult words being, so to say, *more marked*, make a deeper impression upon the mind of the young than the easier ones, and are thus brought almost on a level with the latter.

It is, however, not necessary for the children to copy the " marks " when they copy the words.

Those not at all acquainted with the art of teaching reading, as well as those teachers who think that the highest wisdom in teaching consists in going steadily along an old, well-trodden path of routine, will with difficulty be persuaded that so venerable a method, and one so generally followed as the spelling or alphabetic method is radically wrong and injurious. They know so well, and consider it so natural, that the letters w-h-i-c-h represent the word *which ;* but to children this, as at present pronounced, is a mystery, as great as that a £5 note should represent five sovereigns, *unless they are* TOLD. And in that really all the difference lies. We wish children with their own eyes and with their own intellect to see what they have to learn, and not to make them the passive instruments of their teachers. Besides, we wish to give them while young the pure gold, and make them acquainted with our conventional contrivances when they are old enough to understand them, and also old enough not to be intellectually injured by them.

## INTRODUCTION.

The most natural course in affixing the "marks" to letters having various sounds, appeared to the Author to examine which sound, on any page, occurred most frequently; or which was the *prevailing* sound of each of those letters, and he allowed then the usual letter to stand for that sound, whilst its *varieties*, occurring less frequently, received the "marks."

The *prevailing* sound, for instance, of *a* is that in *man*, and *far* ; the *varieties* which we have are the a in *fare* and that in *war*, and are represented by ā and ạ respectively.

The prevailing sound of *i* is not I, the pronoun, but *i* as it sounds in *will, inn, which*. In the Lord's Prayer, for instance, the letter *i* occurs twenty times, and in only *one* of them it has the *I* sound represented ī; whereas sixteen sound like *i* as in *which, in, kingdom*, &c.

Similarly, the hard sound of *c*, as in *cat*, is the *prevailing* sound; its variety, as in *mice*, is represented c̱.

The following additional remarks are given to enable any teacher previously unacquainted with this method to avail himself of it. Before this little book is placed in the hands of the pupils, the following excercises are recommended :—

### I. *Preparatory Exercises for the Eye and Hand.*

1. Comparison of dots in various positions on the black board to secure that the children have accurate notions of what is meant by "above," "below," "right," "left," &c. Also drawing lines on the board by the teacher to explain such notions as a "straight line" (for horizontal), "upright" (for perpendicular), "slanting," "slanting to the right," "slanting up," "round," "crooked," "half," "quarter," "thick," "thin," &c.

2. Drawing these lines by the pupils on their slates, first with the help of a ruler, a book, or a slip of paper; afterwards, freehand.

The order suggested to be followed is indicated at the commencement of the "Introductory Exercises." Parallel with the above must be practised the—

## II. *Preparatory Exercises for the organs of Speech.*

1. Exercises in *Speaking* and *Pronunciation*, for which object lessons, such as are briefly sketched in the "Easy Reading Lessons," page 56, &c., afford materials.

The object of these exercises is to strengthen the children's organs of speech, to accustom them to a correct pronunciation, and to make them think.

2. Analysis of a piece of poetry *into words, syllables,* and *sounds.*

The pupils should commit to memory the first stanza of the subjoined piece of poetry, the teacher saying line after line slowly and distinctly, and the pupils repeating after him, both in chorus and singly.

Then the teacher should say it again line after line, stopping after every word, the children counting how often he stops, thus *learning* of how many words each line and stanza consists.

They should then say in turn, " Oh " is a word, " I " is a word, " Love " is a word, &c. So with each of the three stanzas. To effect the analysis of the words into *syllables,* the teacher would let the children find out that words, for the utterance of which we have to make only *one* effort, like " Oh," " I," " love," " the," &c., consist of *one* syllable ; while those for the utterance of which we have to make two, three, or more efforts, like, " mer-ry," " sun-shine," " ho-li-day," consist of *two, three,* or more syllables. As in the analysis of the lines into words, the pupils, one after the other, will say of how many syllables each word consists. Lastly, the syllables are resolved into *sounds.* The teacher again, in the

INTRODUCTION.  xiii.

first instance, would pronounce slowly and distinctly a syllable consisting of more than one sound, l-o-ve, when the pupils will have no difficulty in discovering that the word "love" consists of *three sounds*, l-o-ve; the syllable "mer," of the three, "m-e-r;" ry of two, r-y; "sun" of three, s-u-n; "shine" of three, sh-i-ne; "it" of two, i-t; "makes" of four, m-a-ke-s, &c., and so on with every word. In this manner the whole piece of poetry will be analysed into *words, syllables,* and *sounds*. We subjoin the complete analysis into *words, syllables,* and *sounds*, of the piece of poetry. That into words being self-evident, the lines marked (1) indicate the *syllables*, and the lines (2) show the *sounds*.

(1)—Oh, I love the mer-ry sun-shine!
(2)—O, I l-o-v(e) th-e m-e-r-r-y s-u-n–sh-i-n(e)!
(1)—It makes my heart so gay,
(2)—I-t m-a-k-(e)s m-y h-ea-r-t s-o g-ay,
(1)—To hear the sweet birds sing-ing
(2)—T-o h-ea-r th-e s-w-ee-t b-i-r-d-s s-i-ng-i-ng
(1)—On their sum-mer ho-li-day.
(2)—O-n th-ei-r s-u-m-m-e-r h-o-l-i-d-ay.

(1)—Oh, I love the mer-ry sun-shine!
(2)—O, I l-o-v(e) th-e m-e-r-r-y s-u-n-sh-i-n(e)!
(1)—The dew-y mor-ning hour;
(2)—Th-e d-ew-y m-o-r-n-i-ng (h)ou-r;
(1)—With ro-sy smiles ad-van-cing,
(2)—W-i-th r-o-s-y s-m-i-l-(e)s a-d–v-a-n–c-i-ng,
(1)—Like a beau-ty from her bow-er,
(2)—L-i-k(e) a b-eau-t-y f-r-o-m h-e-r b-ow–e-r.

(1)—Oh, it charms the soul from sad-ness,
(2)—O, i-t ch-a-r-m-s th-e s-ou-l f-r-o-m s-a-d–n-e-ss,
(1)—It sets the spi-rit free;
(2)—I-t s-e-t-s th-e s-p-i–r-i-t f-r-ee;
(1)—The sun-shine is all beau-ty,
(2)—Th-e s-u-n–sh-i-n(e) i-s a-ll b-eau–t-y,
(1)—Oh, the mer-ry sun for me.
(2)—O, th-e m-e-r–r-y s-u-n f-o-r m-e.

Teachers not experienced in analysing words into sounds, and who may be diffident in performing the operation with other words, will notice that it really consists in nothing but pronouncing each word so slowly as to render its constituent sounds discernible by detaching the one from the other. And this slow pronunciation is the key, so to say, of the constituent sounds of each word, and can be applied readily by any teacher after a little practice.

The shorter or longer practice of the "Preparatory Exercises," depending entirely upon the degree of mental development of the children to be taught, must be left to the judgment of the teacher, who might even dispense with them almost entirely in teaching a small class of intelligent children. With large classes they have the invaluable advantage of preparing all the pupils so as to secure with most of them rapid progress in the main objects :—

### III. *Reading and Writing.*

In introducing these, the teacher will write on the black board the letter *o*, the pupils copy it, and call it *o*. Then the letter *n* is written on the board, called *n*, not *enn*, and again copied by the children. Then the combinations of these letters *on* and *no* are written on the board, and are read and copied by the children.

After they have thus learned the first lesson in reading and writing *from the board*, then only the little book should be placed in their hands, and they will go over the same lesson again from the book. In a similar manner every other lesson must be treated, following closely the course of the book. It is, however, not necessary for the children to write the *whole of the longer lessons* the first time the course is gone through; the part marked (*a*) only of these lessons may prove sufficient. The rest, marked (*b*), may be written by them when the course is gone through for the second or third time.

From the plan of the work it will be clear that the beginner has only to deal with *one kind of letters* both for *writing and reading*. This has the advantage of avoiding confusion; and until a child has perceived that reading is the easiest and most natural process of the world, nothing ought to be introduced which might prove a stumbling block to him. But it must be left to each teacher to decide whether to postpone the reading of the *second part*, which contains the materials of the first in letter-press characters, until the first is completed, or until the child is about half-way through the first. The rest of the method is sufficiently indicated in the book at the various stages. Children who have mastered this little book can continue their studies by reading any good elementary reading book, by copying, writing from dictation, spelling, &c.

On no account should the pupils be hurried on to the next lesson before they have completely mastered the preceding one. It is also of the utmost importance that the teacher should require his pupils, at an early stage, to connect the sounds of each word one with another, and not to stop after each. They must pronounce in one flow of voice, for instance, the word "wall" just as the letters are connected in writing; and it must be as little permitted to the pupils to read w-a-ll as he would be allowed to write it in that fashion.

As a matter of course the indication of the sounds of the letters before the lessons in the text, as well as the key, are not intended for the pupils, but for the teachers; the key serving only as a kind of index to the sounds, the pupils learn them gradually as they are introduced in the lessons.

Teaching elementary reading and writing is generally considered tedious work to teachers and pupils. Experience has proved that if these most important subjects are treated by the method recommended, and made available by the author, the task of the teachers will be greatly lessened, and the pupils will find amusement and pleasure in their first studies, while, at the same time, their intellect is expanded under the very process of laying the foundation, and of acquiring the most important key to their future studies.

the lambs were ti-red, he used to car-ry them in his arms; and when they were all eat-ing their sup-pers in the field, he used to sit up-on a stile and play them a tune, and sing to them; so they were hap-py sheep and lambs. But al-ways at night the shep-herd used to pen them up in a fold.

Now they were all ve-ry hap-py, as I told you, and lov-ed the shep-herd dear-ly, who was so good to them, all ex-cept one fool-ish lit-tle lamb. And this lamb did not like to be shut up al-ways at night in the fold, so she came to her mo-ther, who was a wise old sheep, and said to her: "I won-der why we are shut up? I think it is ve-ry hard, and I will get a-way if I can, that I will, for I like to run a-bout where I please, and I think it is ve-ry plea-sant in the woods by moon-light."

Then the old sheep said to her: "You are ve-ry sil-ly, you lit-tle lamb, you had bet-ter stay in the fold. The shep-herd is so good to us, that we should al-ways do as he bids us; and if you wan-der a-bout by your-self, I dare say you will come to some harm." "I dare say not," said the lit-tle lamb. And so when the night came, and the shep-herd cal-led them all to come in-to the fold, she would not come, but hid her-self; and when the rest of the lambs were all in the fold, and fast a-sleep, she came out, and jump-ed, and frisk-ed, and danc-ed about; and she got out of the field, and got into a fo-rest, full of trees, and a ve-ry fierce wolf came rush-ing out of a cave and howl-ed ve-ry loud. Then the sil-ly lamb wish-ed she had been shut up in the fold, but the fold was a great way off, and the wolf saw her, and seiz-ed her, and car-ri-ed her away to a dis-mal dark den, spread all o-ver with bones and blood ; and there the wolf had two cubs, and the wolf said to them : " Here, I have brought you a young fat lamb." And so the cubs took her, and grow-led o-ver her a lit-tle while, then tore her to pieces, and ate her up.

### 29.—The Sun.

The sun ris-es in the east ; and when he ris-es it is day. He shines up-on the trees and houses, and up-on the wa-ter ; and ev-e-ry-thing looks spark-ling and beau-ti-ful when he shines up-on it. He gives us light and heat. He makes the fruit ri-pen. If he did not shine up-on the fields, and upon the gar-dens, no-thing would grow.

Some-times he takes off his crown of bright rays, and wraps up his head in thin clouds, and then we may look at him ; but when there are no clouds, and he shines with all his bright-ness at noon, we can-not look at him, for he would daz-zle our eyes, and make us blind ; only the ea-gle can look at him then ; the eagle, with his strong, pierc-ing eye, can look up-on him al-ways. When the sun is go-ing to rise in the morn-ing, and make it day, the lark flies up in the sky to meet him, and sings sweet-ly in the air, and the cock crows loud to tell ev-e-ry bo-dy that he is com-ing; but the owl and the bat fly a-way when they see him, and hide them-selves in old walls and hol-low trees, and the li-on and ti-ger go in-to their caves, where they sleep all the day. The sun shines in all coun-tries, all o-ver the earth. He is one of the most beau-ti-ful and glor-i-ous crea-tures that can be seen in the whole world.

## 30.—The Moon.

The moon shines to give us light in the night, when the sun is set.

She is very beau-ti-ful, and white like sil-ver. We may look at her al-ways, for she is not so bright as to daz-zle our eyes, and she ne-ver scorch-es us. She is mild and gen-tle. She lets even the lit-tle glow-worms shine, which are quite dark by day. The stars shine all round her, but she seems lar-ger and bright-er than the stars, and looks like a large pearl a-mongst a great ma-ny small spark-ling di-a-monds. When you are a-sleep she shines through your cur-tains with her gen-tle beams, and seems to say: "Sleep on, poor lit-tle tir-ed boys, I will not dis-turb you."

The night-in-gale sings to her, and sings bet-ter than all the birds of the air. She sits up-on a thorn, and sings sweet-ly all the night long, while the dew lies up-on the grass, and ev-e-ry thing a-round is still and si-lent.

# SECOND PART. SECTION C.

## PIECES OF POETRY.
TO BE READ, COPIED, AND COMMITTED TO MEMORY.

### 1.—LITTLE THINGS.

Lit-tle drops of wa-ter,
Lit-tle grains of sand
Make the migh-ty o-cean,
And the plea-sant land.

Thus the lit-tle mo-ments,
Hum-ble though they be,
Make the migh-ty a-ges
Of e-ter-ni-ty.

Thus our lit-tle er-rors
Lead the soul a-way
From the path of vir-tue,
Oft in sin to stray.

Lit-tle deeds of kind-ness,
Lit-tle words of love,
Make our earth an E-den,
Like the hea-ven a-bove.

## 2.—HU-MI-LI-TY.

The bird that soars on high-est wing
   Builds on the ground his low-ly nest,
And she that doth most sweet-ly sing
   Sings in the shade, when all things rest:
In lark and night-in-gale we see,
   What hon-our hath hu-mi-li-ty.

## 3.—THE LITTLE BROOK.

You lit-tle brook, so bright and clear,
How glad I am your voice to hear;
I ask you, while I watch you flow,
Whence do you come and whith-er go?

"I come from yon-der rocks' re-cess,
My course goes over moss and cress,
My mir-ror shows to every eye
The friend-ly pic-ture of the sky.

"Thus like a child of mer-ry mind,
I trouble not my way to find;
For He who called me from the stone,
Will be, I trust, my guide alone."

*After Göthe.*

## 4.—GOD'S TEACH-ING.

Who taught the bird to build her nest
Of wool, and hay, and moss?
Who taught her how to weave it best,
And lay the twigs a-cross?

Who taught the busy bee to fly
A-mong the sweet-est flowers,
And lay her store of ho-ney by,
To eat in win-ter hours?

Who taught the lit-le ant the way,
  Her nar-row hole to bore,
And through the pleas-ant sum-mer's day,
  To gath-er up her store?

'Twas God who taught them all the way,
  And gave their lit-tle skill;
Who teach-es child-ren, when they pray,
  To do His holy will.

### 5.—USE OF TIME.

How doth the lit-tle busy bee
Im-prove each shin-ing hour,
And ga-ther honey all the day,
From every opening flower.

How skilfully she builds her cell!
How neat she spreads her wax!
And labours hard to store it well
With the sweet food she makes.

In works of labour or of skill
I would be busy too;
For Satan finds some mischief still
For idle hands to do.

In books, or work, or health-ful play,
    Let my first years be past,
That I may give, for every day,
    Some good account at last.

### 6.—MOR-NING HYMN.

I thank Thee, Lord, for qui-et rest,
    And for Thy care of me ;
Oh! let me through this day be blest,
    And kept from harm by Thee.

Oh! let me love Thee ; kind Thou art
    To chil-dren such as I ;
Give me a gen-tle, holy heart,
    Be Thou my friend on high.

### 7.—EVE-NING HYMN.

Now the sun has passed away,
With the golden light of day ;
Now the shades of si-lent night,
Hide the flow-ers from our sight.
Now the little stars on high,
Twinkle in the mighty sky.

Father, mer-ci-ful and mild,
Listen to Thy little child ;
Loving Father put away
All things wrong I've done to-day ;

Make me gentle, true, and good,
Make me love Thee as I should;
Make me feel by day and night,
I am ever in Thy sight.

Jesus was a little child,
Make me like Him meek and mild.
Heav-en-ly Father, hear my prayer,
Take Thy child unto Thy care.
Let Thy angels good and bright,
Watch around me through the night;
Keep me now, and when I die,
Take me to the glo-ri-ous sky.
Father, mer-ci-ful and mild,
Listen to Thy little child.

### 8.—WE ARE SEVEN;

#### OR A CHILD'S NOTION OF DEATH.

A sim-ple child
That light-ly draws its breath,
And feels its life in ev-ery limb,
What should it know of death?

I met a lit-le cot-tage girl,
She was eight years old, she said;
Her hair was thick with many a curl
That clus-ter-ed round her head.

She had a rus-tic wood-land air,
    And she was wild-ly clad :
Her eyes were fair, and very fair,
    Her beauty made me glad.

"Sis-ters and broth-ers, lit-le maid,
    How many may you be ?"
"How many ? Sev-en in all," she said,
    And, won-der-ing look-ed at me.

" And where are they ? I pray you tell."
    She answered, " Seven are we ;
And two of us at Con-way dwell,
    And two are gone to sea.

" Two of us in the church-yard lie,
    My sis-ter and my broth-er ;
And in the church-yard cot-tage, I
    Dwell near them with my moth-er.

" You say that two at Con-way dwell,
    And two are gone to sea ;
Yet you are sev-en !—I pray you tell,
    Sweet maid, how this may be."

Then did the lit-tle maid reply,
    " Sev-en boys and girls are we ;
Two of us in the church-yard lie,
    Beneath the church-yard tree."

"You run a-bout, my little maid,
  Your limbs they are a-live;
If two are in the church-yard laid,
  Then you are only five."

"Their graves are green, they may be seen,"
  The little maid re-pli-ed,
"Twelve steps or more from my moth-er's door,
  And they are side by side.

"My stock-ings there I of-ten knit,
  My ker-chief there I hem;
And there up-on the ground I sit—
  I sit and sing to them.

"And, of-ten af-ter sun-set, Sir,
  When it is light and fair,
I take my lit-tle por-rin-ger,
  And eat my sup-per there.

"The first that died was lit-tle Jane;
  In bed she moan-ing lay,
Till God re-leased her of her pain,
  And then she went a-way.

"So in the church-yard she was laid;
  And all the sum-mer day
To-geth-er round her grave we play-ed,
  My bro-ther John and I.

"And when the ground was white with snow,
  And I could run and slide,
My brother John was forced to go,
  And he lies by her side."

"How many are you then," said I,
  "If there are two in hea-ven?"
The lit-tle mai-den did re-ply,
  "O, mas-ter! we are sev-en."

"But they are dead; those two are dead,
  Their spir-its are in heav-en!"
'Twas throw-ing words a-way; for still
  The lit-tle maid would have her will,
And said, "Nay, we are sev-en."

                      *Wordsworth.*

# MAST'S

# PHONIC METHOD OF TEACHING READING AND WRITING SIMULTANEOUSLY.

*Extracts from the "Educational Times," Jan.* 1, 1875, containing opinions expressed on the author's method, in a discussion that followed the reading of his paper at the College of Preceptors, in December, 1874.

"Dr. GLADSTONE thought that the easy passage of the child[*] before them from the phonetic to the unphonetic part of her exercise, was very striking testimony to the truth and value of the system employed in her instruction."

"Prof. PAYNE said that the reading difficulty presented a curious puzzle in a most important subject. Dr. Morell stated that he could count on his fingers the schools in which really good results had been, to his knowledge, obtained in the matter of intonation and proper expression. . . . . In the illustrations brought before them, one of the most valuable testimonials to the system was the hesitation now and then shown by the child,[*] which proved that she was thinking, not learning to become a machine. Thus she had been prepared to gain independent results, while a child differently trained would have only mechanical helps to rely upon, and hence would make no further spontaneous advances, not having laid up a store of self-activity as under an intelligent system of instruction. . . . . The child referred to had really learned to read; all she now needed was practice. It was not necessary that the child should be at once plunged into all the difficulties of language; its experience of life would remove them as they arose, if the principles had been fully comprehended."

"Dr. OPPLER, having tried many methods, had been driven to take refuge in the system well known in Germany as the *Lautir Methode*, with which Mr. Mast's had some points of agreement, though on the whole superior to it. He held that the character of a pupil's reading, in the secondary or later stages of his training, afforded a standpoint from which the whole merit and effect of his education could be gauged; so many branches of mental acquisition were implied in really good reading. Proper training in this subject awakened in the child's mind the imaginative, retentive, and combining faculties. There was very much in the winning manner of the teacher, of which they had just seen an example. He agreed with Quintilian that nothing should be excluded which would stimulate or invite the child in learning to read: " Vel si quid aliud quo magis illa aetas gaudeat, inveniri potest, quod tractare, intueri, nominare, jucundum sit."

---

[*] The allusions refer to a girl, six years of age, after having been taught by the author less than three months, in lessons lasting 10 to 15 minutes daily. Now, after nine months' instruction, she can read any book within the scope of young children, and at the same time she can *read* and answer the letters received from her young friends.

*By the same Author.*

# LINEAR DRAWING:

AN INTRODUCTION TO TECHNICAL DRAWING, CONSISTING OF 24 PLATES (4 COLOURED), CONTAINING 100 FIGURES, GEOMETRICAL, ORNAMENTAL, ARCHITECTURAL, ENGINEERING, MECHANICAL, &c., AND A

## TEXT BOOK,

GIVING COMPREHENSIVE EXPLANATIONS FOR THE CONSTRUCTION OF THE FIGURES AND NUMEROUS EXERCISES.

*Price: Set of Plates, 4/-   Text Book, 1/-*

Henry Weekes, Esq., R.A., expressed himself as follows on the work :—

"I have examined the Text and Plates of your new work on Linear Drawing, and can, without hesitation, say that your object is a good one, as I understand it, namely, to lead a pupil through elementary geometry into ornamental design.

"Few of our youths have hitherto been taught the immense value of the rule and compasses, and to what extent shapes of the most fanciful kind may be produced by them alone.

"The old gothic architects were great masters in the use of them, and hence the many beautiful forms we find in their works, combined with sound architectural constructiveness. The study of Linear Drawing of this kind, whilst it made them profound geometricians, led them gradually into art of a higher nature, and the consequence was that, when their hand was guided by the eye alone, it never departed from what was expressive both of beauty and fitness. Their line and rule, or, in other words, their geometrical knowledge, unconsciously governed their fancies, and so prevented them from becoming wild and absurd.

"Every man should, in my opinion, be a geometrician, whether he be brought in contact with art or not, as it tends to give him that proper balance of mind necessary to sound thinking of all kinds.

"Allow me to congratulate you on taking a step in the right direction, and to wish you all the success your attempt, so well carried out, deserves."

### Opinions of the Press.

"'During an experience of upwards of twenty years in the work of education in this country,' says the author of this little work, 'I have often felt the want of a good introduction to *linear drawing* for schools.' Existing books were either too advanced, and suitable only for some trade or profession, or too elementary and uninstructive. Mr. Mast has supplied the deficiency, and in a manner that will be generally approved and admired; for his instructions are clear and simple, and they are accompanied with 100 illustrations, every one of which has its particular use, and is designed with judicious thoughtfulness, ascending from the straight line and its divisions to geometrical designs of remarkable elegance and beauty. All this is rendered so plainly, and shown to be so easy, that both boys and girls will derive pleasure as well as instruction from the study, feeling at every step the progress they are making from elementary geometry to the richness of ornamental] design. Mr. Mast deserves great praise for having produced a work of so much use and interest."—*The News of the World, Jan. 25, 1874.*

"To diffuse sound technical information among the people, and thereby advance the cultivation of the arts, fine and mechanical, and to improve the national taste and genius, has been recognised as an essential part of education, hitherto uncared for in this country, no longer to be neglected. But how best to diffuse that information systematically, and in a form to produce the most certain practical results, is a subject of much controversy. The author of the work before us has, we think, gone a considerable way to solve the problem. His lengthened experience as head master of a London school, the Belgrave College, and his knowledge of the mode of imparting technical instruction in the seminaries of Germany, have enabled him to understand clearly the wants of the English course of teaching, and to supply them from German sources. Mr. Mast has composed his Text Book, and prepared his Series of Drawings—24 plates (4 coloured), containing 100 figures, geometrical, ornamental, architectural, mechanical, &c.—designed for the use of schools and private students, and which, in our opinion, admirably carries out the author's intention. That the design of the work, as a grammar of drawing, is commendable, and the execution of it good, cannot be questioned, for it comes before the public stamped with the approbation of the eminent sculptor and Royal Academician, Mr. Henry Weekes."—*Civil Service Gazette, Feb. 14, 1874.*

"He (Mr. Mast) does not ask that the usual process should be reversed, he only begs for the cultivation of linear drawing side by side with free-hand drawing, and hence he has produced a work consisting of a text-book and an elaborate and carefully prepared set of plates, whereby the student who has received no intimation whatever into drawing may begin with lines and instruments. His linear drawing is therefore more elementary than usual; it is in a measure a first introduction to the whole art of drawing. We think Mr. Mast is right. A superior facility and quality of freehand work may be expected where exactness and the right use of instruments have been taught. Mr. Mast publishes his excellent little work as a contribution towards that technical education about which this country is becoming so anxious, lest we should be passed in the race of manufacture by our foreign competitors. So he hopes that his Linear Drawing will be introduced into the higher class of Board schools, and we hope so too.—*The School Board Chronicle, Feb. 14, 1874.*

"LINEAR DRAWING.—In a little book under the above title, accompanied by a portfolio of photograhs, the author, Mr. G. Christian Mast, has made a praiseworthy and successful effort to produce a really useful handbook for elementary students. He has developed further in this little work than in any other of similar pretensions that we have seen, the combination of geometrical figures in ornamental design, the analyses of which are given clearly in the handbook.—*Engineering, April 24, 1874.*

"By its publication the author has supplied a want which teachers have long felt—a really good introduction to Linear Drawing for schools. The pupil is led, by it, in a series of simple and progressive stages, through the elements of geometrical drawing to the construction of elaborate designs, with comparatively little help from the teacher. It will therefore be found invaluable in introducing drawing into schools where it has not hitherto been studied from the want of competent masters.—*West Middlesex Advertiser, May 30, 1874.*

LONDON: C. BEAN, 81, NEW NORTH ROAD.

*Price One Shilling.*

## "FRENCH: PRACTICE AND THEORY."
### BY G. C. MAST.

May be obtained from the Author at the following prices :—Single copies, 1s. ; 6 copies, 5s. ; 12 copies, 9s. 6d. ; 25 copies, 19s.

---

The following are extracts from Reviews of this work :—

"Among other educational works of a high class lately published, we may mention the excellent treatise on "French—Practice and Theory," by G. C. Mast (Bean, New North-road, London). Small in bulk and unpretending in style, this volume quite bears out the character which its author claims for it, as embodying a new, practical, and natural method of learning to speak and to write the French language. The arrangement is clear and simple, and the exercises comprehensive as well as lucid."—*The Daily Telegraph, May* 12, 1873.

"Mr. G. C. Mast has discovered a happy method of making instruction in the French language both certain and pleasing. . . . . This little book well deserves the attention of educationalists, and also of persons desirous of instructing themselves in the French language, to whom it will afford certain and pleasant assistance."—*The News of the World, Oct.* 6, 1872.

"This is an admirable little book. The phrases, such as are in daily use, are adapted to the capacity of juvenile students, and grammatical rules are blended with familiar conversation. . . . . . The book is well printed and published at a very reasonable price."—*The Civil Service Gazette, Oct.* 12, 1872.

"Mr. Mast has achieved a triumph. Successful and experienced as a teacher, he has turned his experience to good account. In contradistinction to the synthetic method of teaching adopted by Ollendorf and others, by which the structure of the language is dissolved into its elements, Mr. Mast retains its structure in its integrity, and teaches his pupils to observe what is most beautiful and useful in the various parts of the fabric, and then with the model still present before their eyes trains them to imitate the perfections they have admired. This little treatise will be found a valuable help and service to teachers and pupils." . . . . . .—*The English Churchman and Clerical Journal, Nov.* 14, 1872.

"The first thing Mr. Mast asks his young pupils to do on their introduction to French, is to learn about a dozen French phrases, 'Ouvrez la porte,' 'Entrez,' 'Pourquoi,' 'Il fait froid,' Dites moi,' &c. Long experience has convinced him that this is a better beginning than 'ah,' 'ba,' 'sa,' 'da.' On the face of it the method is reasonable, and when it comes as the direct result of the author's twenty or thirty years' experience as a teacher of French in England and Germany, it commends itself as a plan well worthy of the attention of all teachers of French in our schools. . . . . We look with interest for Mr. Mast's plan of dealing with the Accidence. 'Practic and Theory' promises to be a valuable assistance to both teacher and pupil."— *The School Board Chronicle, Feb.* 8, 1873.

---

LONDON · CHARLES BEAN, 81, NEW NORTH ROAD.

www.ingramcontent.com/pod-product-compliance
Lightning Source LLC
Chambersburg PA
CBHW021943160426
43195CB00011B/1208